I0005042

Computers for K
Something In, Something Out

by David Schwartzberg

photography by Pacha Mongkolwongrojn

To my wife for her patience

and my two inspirations, Sammy and Max.

This edition published in the USA by

Scruff Daddy Productions

2405 Brian Drive, Northbrook, IL 60062

Writing and graphic design by David Schwartzberg

Photography by Pacha Mongkolwongrojn

Copyright © 2011 by Scruff Daddy Productions, Northbrook, Illinois

ISBN 978-0-578-09195-2

No part of this publication may be reproduced, stored in a retrieval system or transmitted in any form or by any means, electronic, mechanical, photocopying, recording, scanning or otherwise, except as permitted under Sections 107 or 108 of the 1976 United States Copyright Act, without the prior written permission of the Publisher.

SCRUFF DADDY PRODUCTIONS

ALL RIGHTS RESERVED 2011

This is
Sammy.

Sammy has two **computers**. He uses a **PC** and an **iPod Touch**.

PC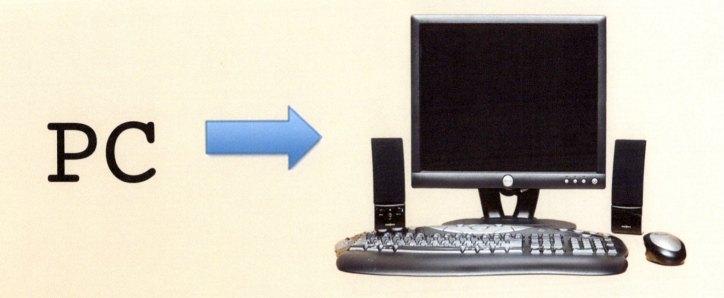

  iPod
Touch

Sammy enjoys using a **computer** for games and learning.

The **iPod Touch** is a pocket-sized **computer** that uses your finger to tell it what to do. That's called **input**!

Making gestures
like **tapping,**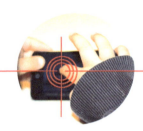
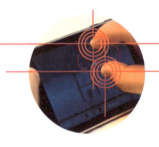 **pinching**
or **sliding**
sends input to the
iPod Touch.

It's okay to pinch your iPod Touch,

but not your little brother!

The **PC** is a desktop sized **computer** that uses a **keyboard** and a **mouse** for **input**.

PC

Does this
mouse
have a
tail?

mice

The **keyboard** has keys with letters, numbers, words or **symbols**.

You press a key to send **input** to the computer.

Remember to curl your fingers.

A computer **mouse** uses a **pointer** to tell you where it is on the **display**. The **display** uses pictures and windows to show you what the **computer** is doing.

display

output

That's called
output!

This is the Safari web browser on Mac OS X

iPad

Zoom

Minimize

Close

Address Bar

Search Bar

Some windows can look different

but they help you just the same.

Close

Maximize

Address Bar   Search Bar   Minimize

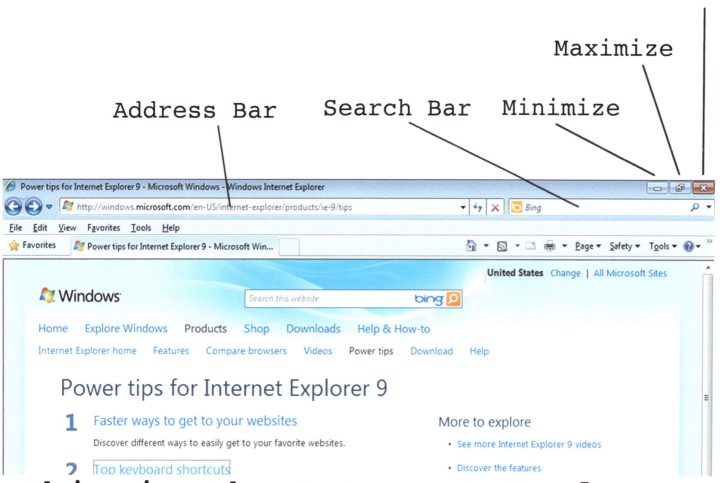

This is the Internet Explorer (IE) web browser on Windows 7

Sammy moves and **clicks** the **mouse** by pressing its buttons to send **input**.

Clicking twice
quickly is called

double-clicking.

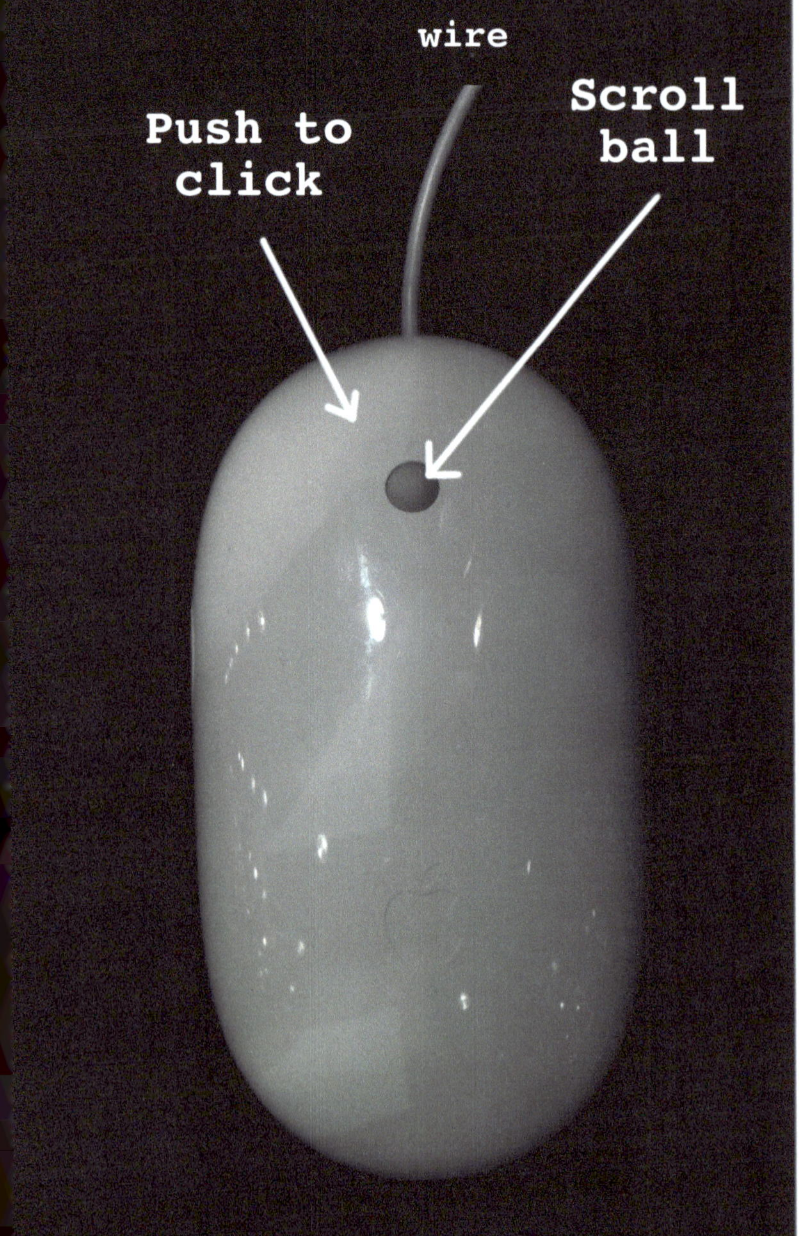

wire

Push to click

Scroll ball

Push to click

Scroll wheel

one-button mouse (wired)

two-button mouse (wireless)

Mice can have one or more buttons.

If Sammy sends **input** by touching, pressing or **double-clicking**, then the **computer** gives **output**.

Sammy can also print from his **PC**. He doesn't like to waste paper. Sammy will reuse or **recycle** scrap paper.

Pass It On!

Image from epa.gov

Joysticks are used to play video games.

Moving the stick and pressing buttons
sends input. It's also a lot of fun!

Input can come from a pen and pad, just like writing on paper or coloring. This has large buttons for input too.

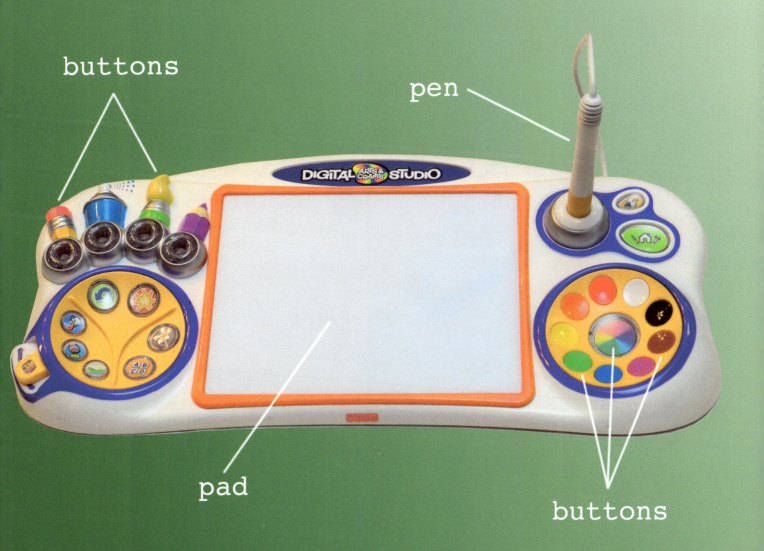

buttons

pen

pad

buttons

Sometimes we need to wait our turn and share the **computer**. It's especially nice to share with people we love.

Glossary

Address Bar >_

This is the long rectangle in a web browser where you can type a web site name. The web site address usually starts with www, but doesn't have to.

Click >_

A way to give a computer input using a mouse. The input you give the computer usually tells it to select something for you by pressing a button once and releasing.

Close button >_

A button found in the upper-right or upper-left corner of a window in a computer. This button will shutdown the open computer program until opened again.

Computers >_

Machines that are very good at doing math over and over again without making a mistake. Computers can be used for work, games, learning and even help your family car.

Display >_

One part of the computer that shows you what the computer is doing, called output. A display is also called a monitor or the screen.

Double-clicking >_

A way to give a computer input using a mouse. The input you give the computer usually tells it to select something for you by pressing a button twice quickly.

Gestures >_

To give the computer input using your fingers. Some gestures are tapping, sliding and pinching.

iPod Touch >_

A small handheld computer with a display you touch.

Input >_

Telling a computer what you want it to do using something like a mouse, a keyboard, a joystick or your fingers.

Keyboard >_

Part of the computer that has buttons with letters, number and symbols you press to tell the computer what to do. The keyboard also has some keys with words such as 'enter', 'return' and 'delete'.

Keyboard, wireless >_

This keyboard connects to the computer without using a cable. It connects to the computer using radio signals.

Mac OS X >_

MacIntosh or Mac computers use the Mac OS X operating system to control parts of the computer and run programs.

Maximize button >_

This button is on the top of the window and its job is to make the window as big as the display.

Minimize button >_

This button is on the top of the windows and its job is to make the window to go sleep without closing it.

Mouse >_

Part of the computer that is moved around by your hand to guide the pointer. A mouse has one or more buttons for clicking.

Mouse, wireless >_

This mouse connects to the computer without using a cable. It connects to the computer using invisible signals.

Output >_

Something a computer does or shows you on a monitor after you tell it what to do.

PC >_

This is short for the letters used for Personal Computers.

Pinch or Pinching >_

A gesture to tell your iPod Touch, iPhone or iPad to grow or shrink what you are looking at.

Pointer >_

for example a link pointer
Usually an arrow, but doesn't have to be, that you control to move around the display. The arrow helps you know where the mouse thinks it is.

Recycle >_

The steps taken to change some garbage into something new and useful again.

Scroll ball >_

Part of the mouse that uses a gentle touch from your finger to give input to a window.

Scroll wheel >_

Part of the mouse that uses a wheel to give input to a window, such as scrolling up and down.

Search Bar >_

An area that looks like a rectangle in a window or web browser where you can type words to search.

Single-Clicking >_

See click.

Sliding >_

A gesture to tell your iPod Touch, iPhone or iPad to move a switch or level change a setting or open something.

Symbols >_

Text symbols on computers can be inputted with the use of keyboard. They are meaningful shapes that computers can use for commands.

Tapping >_

A gesture to tell your iPod Touch, iPhone or iPad to do something like open an app.

Windows XP or Windows 7 >_

PC computers use the Windows operating system to control parts of the computer and run programs.

Zoom >_

This button is at the top of the windows and its job is to make the window get closer to what you are looking at.

www.ingramcontent.com/pod-product-compliance
Lightning Source LLC
Chambersburg PA
CBHW041424050326
40689CB00002B/651